I'd love to hear your stories, because they made you who you are today!

To:_____

With Love, From: _____

"Sometimes you never know the value of a moment until it becomes a memory." – Dr. Seuss.

Memoir Mastery

A Step-by-Step Guide to Writing Your Life Story

SYDNEY BROWN

Memoir Mastery

by Sydney Brown

Published by TLM Publishing House

5905 Atlanta Highway, Alpharetta GA.
https://www.ttpublishinghouse.com
Copyright © 2023 TLM Publishing House

Acknowledgment

I want to shout out to my team. While the names have changed over the years, I'm blessed to have the support of skilled people!

Thanks to my *I'm the Writer enrollees*, maiden class, Frances Youngblood, Grace A Missouri, Elecca Maxwell, and Brookelan Ables for helping brainstorm the questions and pain points that writers go through as they delve into the unknown genres!

Preface

Greetings! I hope this book has found its way to you at the perfect time in your life for it to do the absolute most good for you, your life, and others.

Others? You might ask.

For sure! Do you realize people who lack social support are more likely to experience stress and burnout?[1]

Also, according to a survey by the American Psychological Association, stress levels in the US have increased significantly in recent years, with more than half of Americans citing stress as a significant problem.[2]

What's worse, the suicide rate is higher among individuals who feel isolated and disconnected from

---

[1] Cohen, S. (2004). Social relationships and health. American Psychologist, 59(8), 676-684.
[2] American Psychological Association. (2017). Stress in America: The State of Our Nation. Retrieved from https://www.apa.org/news/press/releases/stress/2016/state-nation.pdf

others, including those who lack support from mentors or loved ones.[3]

Now, I don't want to put pressure on you to save the world, but you should know there are many people out there who ache for someone to help them through rough times. Your story could be just what someone is looking for. When we feel we have nowhere to turn but don't want to give up, we often turn to books.

Author Matt Haig has credited reading books with helping him through his struggles with depression. In his memoir "Reasons to Stay Alive," he writes: "Books saved me. They still do. They are the cheapest and most accessible form of therapy I know. They are a refuge."

In her book "The Vagina Monologues," Eve Ensler writes about a survivor of sexual violence who found solace and strength in reading books: "Every book she read became a bible to her. She found the words to describe what she had lived through, what she was feeling."

In an interview with The New York Times, author Cheryl Strayed credited reading books with helping her

---

[3] Cacioppo, J. T., & Hawkley, L. C. (2003). Social isolation and health, with an emphasis on underlying mechanisms. Perspectives in Biology and Medicine, 46(3), S39-S52.

through a difficult time in her life: "I started reading books that I knew would help me. I knew that if I read books about women who had been through hard things and survived, that it would help me to believe that I could survive too."

In his book "The Seven Storey Mountain," Thomas Merton writes about how reading books by spiritual writers such as St. Augustine and St. John of the Cross helped him find a sense of purpose and direction in his life.

In her book "Educated," Tara Westover writes about how reading books played a crucial role in her journey to escape her abusive and isolated upbringing: "Reading was my education. I read everything I could get my hands on. Every book I read was a way out."

Trust me, I could go on. I'm unsure if you're reading this book to learn how to write your own memoir for personal reasons so that you can help others—or if you're reaching out to find a way to push through your own internal demons right now. Regardless, I'm here to help as much as I can.

First things first, I invite you to follow my YouTube channel, which has free content (even some free full courses) if you enjoy the audible or conversational method of listening and learning.

Subscribe at:
https://www.youtube.com/@justsydneybrown

Additionally, we have a free writing community for you to join and stay involved with the best content and an opportunity to make more friends with similar interests.

Join at: https://www.facebook.com/groups/aspiring

You can find me across most social media at @JustSydneyBrown. I look forward to hearing from you!

Now that you know how to reach me, let's return to your motivation in taking this journey. Truly, each person might sit down to begin their journey for a different reason. Each and every reason is entirely valid.

I'm going to share with you the 100 top reasons you might be ready to start your personal memoir! If you agree, I challenge you to engage with the group, watch the videos, and get started!

100 Reasons You Should Write Your Personal Memoir Now

You want to:

1. ... preserve your family history for future generations.
2. ... share your life story with loved ones.
3. ... reflect on and process your past experiences.
4. ... make sense of difficult or traumatic events.
5. ... provide inspiration and hope for others.
6. ... explore your personal identity and sense of self.
7. ... honor the memory of loved ones who have passed away.
8. ... find closure after a significant life event.
9. ... gain a better understanding of your emotions and thoughts.
10. ... share life lessons and wisdom with others.
11. ... celebrate your accomplishments and milestones.
12. ... leave a legacy for future generations.
13. ... connect with others who have had similar experiences.
14. ... improve your writing and storytelling skills.
15. ... gain a sense of accomplishment and pride in your life story.
16. ... process and heal from past relationships.
17. ... share your perspective on historical events or cultural trends.
18. ... challenge common stereotypes or misconceptions.
19. ... provide a voice for marginalized communities or underrepresented groups.
20. ... document your personal growth and development.
21. ... provide a resource for researchers or historians.
22. ... share your personal struggles with mental health or addiction.

48. ... explore your experiences with architecture or design.
49. ... document your experiences with spirituality or religion.
50. ... share your experiences with politics or government.
51. ... explore your experiences with science or technology.
52. ... document your experiences with literature or writing.
53. ... explore your experiences with art or visual media.
54. ... explore your experiences with philosophy or spirituality.
55. ... document your experiences with entertainment or media consumption.
56. ... share your experiences with social interactions or relationships.
57. ... explore your experiences with social media or online communities.
58. ... document your experiences with sports or outdoor activities.
59. ... explore your experiences with work or career.
60. ... document your experiences with hobbies or leisure activities.
61. ... share your experiences with travel or adventure.
62. ... explore your experiences with education or learning.
63. ... document your experiences with healthcare or medical treatments.
64. ... share your experiences with relationships, such as friendships or mentorships.
65. ... explore your experiences with spirituality or belief systems.
66. ... document your experiences with social issues or movements.
67. ... share your experiences with communities, such as online communities or support groups.
68. ... explore your experiences with cultures or subcultures.
69. ... document your experiences with business or entrepreneurship.
70. ... share your experiences with activism or advocacy.

71. ... explore your experiences with nature or environmentalism.
72. ... document your experiences with parenting or caregiving.
73. ... share your experiences with learning or personal growth.
74. ... explore your experiences with innovation or invention.
75. ... document your experiences with spiritual practices or meditation.
76. ... share your experiences with art or music appreciation.
77. ... explore your experiences with social norms or expectations.
78. ... document your experiences with belief systems or worldviews.
79. ... share your experiences with social classes or economic statuses.
80. ... explore your experiences with mental or emotional health.
81. ... document your experiences with physical health or wellness.
82. ... share your experiences with sexuality or sexual orientation.
83. ... explore your experiences with creativity or imagination.
84. ... document your experiences with spirituality or faith communities.
85. ... share your experiences with personal growth or development.
86. ... explore your experiences with cultural identity or heritage.
87. ... document your experiences with leadership or teamwork.
88. ... share your experiences with historical events or social movements.
89. ... explore your experiences with social skills or communication.
90. ... document your experiences with interpersonal relationships or dynamics.
91. ... share your experiences with social support or community building.

92. ... explore your experiences with professional development or career growth.
93. ... document your experiences with communication or self-expression.
94. ... share your experiences with hobbies or interests.
95. ... explore your experiences with technological advancements or innovations.
96. ... document your experiences with spiritual practices or religious traditions.
97. ... share your experiences with philosophical or ethical questions.
98. ... explore your experiences with social institutions or systems.
99. ... document your experiences with creative expression or artistic forms.
100. ... explore your experiences with literature or writing.

Which ones apply most to you? Come introduce yourself in the free group and tell me your 'why' for your personal memoir!

And now, forward!

Table of Contents

Introduction to Memoir Writing

What is a memoir?

Ah, the memoir. It's a funny little genre, isn't it? It's like a biography but with more feelings and fewer footnotes. At its core, a memoir is a nonfiction book that tells the story of someone's life experiences. It's like taking a walk in their shoes, but without the blisters.

Memoirs are all about emotions. They're about the highs and lows of life, the joys and the sorrows, the love, and the heartbreak. They're like a rollercoaster ride through someone's life, complete with twists and turns, ups and downs, and maybe even a few loop-de-loops.

But here's the thing about memoirs: they're not just about one person's life. They're about the human experience, about what it means to be alive in this crazy world. Memoirs remind us that we're all in this together, that we all have our struggles and triumphs, and that our stories are worth sharing.

Memoirs can be hilarious, like David Sedaris's "Me Talk Pretty One Day," which recounts his adventures in learning French and living in Paris. They can be heartbreaking, like Joan Didion's "The Year of Magical Thinking," which tells the story of her grief after her husband's sudden death. They can be inspiring, like Michelle Obama's "Becoming," which details her journey from a working-class family on the South Side of Chicago to becoming the First Lady of the United States.

But no matter what the subject, memoirs are all about honesty. They're about telling the truth, even if it's uncomfortable or embarrassing. Memoirs aren't about sugarcoating the past, but about facing it head-on and learning from it.

So, if you're thinking about writing a memoir, go for it! It's a chance to share your story with the world, to connect with others who may be going through similar experiences, and to reflect on what it means to be alive. Just remember to be honest, to be brave, and to have fun along the way.

Why Write a Memoir?

First and foremost, writing a memoir is a chance to take control of your story. It's an opportunity to tell your story in your own words, on your own terms, and to share it with the world. So often in life, we're told what our story is, or we feel like we're living someone else's story. Writing a memoir is a way to claim your own narrative and to say, "This is who I am, and this is what I've been through."

Writing a memoir is also a chance to reflect on your past and to learn from it. By looking back on your life experiences, you can gain insights into yourself and into the world around you. You can see how far you've come, what you've learned, and what you still want to accomplish. Memoirs can be a way of making sense of the world, of understanding our place in it, and of finding meaning in our experiences.

Another reason to write a memoir is to connect with others. Memoirs can be a powerful tool for empathy and understanding. By sharing our stories, we can help others feel less alone, less isolated, and less misunderstood. We can create a sense of community and belonging, and we can learn from the experiences of others. Memoirs can be a way of fostering compassion, of breaking down barriers, and of building bridges between people.

Finally, writing a memoir is a chance to leave a legacy. By putting your story down on paper, you're creating something that will last beyond your lifetime. You're leaving a record of your experiences, your thoughts, and your emotions that can be passed down to future generations. You're contributing to the ongoing human conversation, and you're leaving a mark that will endure.

Writing a memoir is a chance to claim your own narrative, to reflect on your past and learn from it, to connect with others, and to leave a legacy. It's a meaningful and rewarding experience that can help you find purpose, meaning, and connection in your life.

Writing a memoir can be a form of therapy. Sometimes, the act of putting our thoughts and feelings down on paper can be cathartic and healing. Writing a memoir can help us process difficult emotions, confront painful memories, and find closure. It can be a way of transforming our pain into something meaningful and metamorphic.

Writing a memoir can also be a way of honoring the people who have shaped our lives. Whether it's a parent, a friend, a mentor, or a role model, there are likely people in your life who have had a profound impact on who you are today. Writing a memoir can be a way of paying tribute to those individuals, of acknowledging their influence, and of thanking them for the role they've played in your life.

Finally, writing a memoir is an opportunity to grow and evolve as a person. By reflecting on your past experiences, you can gain insights into yourself and into the world around you. You can see where you've made mistakes, where you've succeeded, and where you still have room to grow. Writing a memoir can be a way of setting goals for yourself, of creating a vision for your future, and of taking steps towards the person you want to be.

In short, writing a memoir can be a form of therapy, a way of honoring the people who have shaped us, and an opportunity for personal growth and transformation. It's a chance to tell our stories, to connect with others, and to leave a legacy. So, if you've been thinking about writing a memoir, I encourage you to take the leap. You never know what you might discover along the way.

Examples of famous memoirs

There are so many amazing memoirs out there that have captured the hearts and minds of readers around the world. Here are just a few of the most well-known and beloved memoirs:

1. "The Glass Castle" by Jeannette Walls - This memoir tells the story of Walls' tumultuous childhood growing up with parents who were often neglectful and sometimes abusive. Despite the hardships she faced, Walls went on to become a successful journalist and author, and her memoir is a powerful testament to the human spirit.

2. "Angela's Ashes" by Frank McCourt - This memoir chronicles McCourt's impoverished childhood in Limerick, Ireland, and his struggles to overcome poverty, illness, and a difficult family life. Despite the many obstacles he faced, McCourt went on to become a beloved teacher and writer, and his memoir is a poignant and unforgettable tribute to the resilience of the human spirit.

3. "Wild" by Cheryl Strayed - This memoir tells the story of Strayed's solo hike along the Pacific Crest Trail, which she embarked on after the death of her mother and the dissolution of her marriage. Along the way, she confronts physical and emotional challenges that force

her to confront her own demons and find a way forward.

4. "Born a Crime" by Trevor Noah - This memoir tells the story of Noah's childhood growing up in apartheid South Africa, where he was born to a black mother and a white father at a time when such relationships were illegal. Despite the many obstacles he faced, Noah went on to become a successful comedian and television host, and his memoir is a powerful testament to the human spirit and the power of humor.

5. "The Year of Magical Thinking" by Joan Didion - This memoir tells the story of Didion's grief after the sudden death of her husband, as well as her attempts to come to terms with her own mortality. It's a powerful and deeply moving meditation on love, loss, and the human experience.

6. "I Know Why the Caged Bird Sings" by Maya Angelou - This memoir tells the story of Angelou's childhood growing up in the segregated South, and her struggles with racism, trauma, and abuse. Despite the hardships she faced, Angelou went on to become a celebrated author, poet, and civil rights activist, and her memoir is a powerful testament to the resilience of the human spirit.

7. "Hunger" by Roxane Gay - This memoir explores Gay's relationship with her body, as well as her experiences with sexual assault, trauma, and identity. It's a powerful and honest examination of what it means to live in a world that often seems determined to undermine our sense of self-worth.

8. "Educated" by Tara Westover - This memoir tells the story of Westover's upbringing in a strict, survivalist family in rural Idaho, and her journey to gain an education and escape the confines of her upbringing. It's a powerful testament to the transformative power of education, as well as a sobering examination of the dangers of extremism and isolation.

9. "The Immortal Life of Henrietta Lacks" by Rebecca Skloot - This memoir explores the story of Henrietta Lacks, an African American woman whose cancer cells were used without her knowledge or consent to develop some of the most important medical breakthroughs of the 20th century. It's a powerful and thought-provoking examination of issues of race, consent, and medical ethics.

10. "The Liars' Club" by Mary Karr - This memoir tells the story of Karr's childhood growing up in East Texas, and her struggles to come to terms with a dysfunctional family, poverty, and mental illness. It's a poignant and darkly humorous examination of what it means to

survive in a world that often seems determined to tear us apart.

These memoirs, along with many others, have touched the hearts and minds of readers around the world. They're powerful and honest examinations of the human experience and a testament to the transformative power of storytelling.

Finding Your Theme and Focus

Importance of a Central Theme

Let me tell you, having a central theme in your memoir is like having a compass to guide you through the crazy maze of your life experiences. It's like a lighthouse in a storm, a beacon that shines through the fog and helps you make sense of it all.

A central theme is what gives your memoir focus, purpose, and direction. It's the thread that ties all of your life experiences together and the glue that holds your story together. Without a central theme, your memoir would be like a jigsaw puzzle with no edges - lots of interesting pieces, but no clear picture.

But here's the thing: finding your central theme isn't always easy. It's like trying to find a needle in a haystack, or a matching sock in the dryer. It takes time, patience, and a willingness to dig deep and explore the nooks and crannies of your life experiences.

One way to find your central theme is to ask yourself, "What's the story I want to tell?" Is it a story of resilience in the face of adversity? A story of overcoming fear and doubt? A story of finding love in unexpected places? Whatever it is, your central theme should be something that speaks to the heart of your story, and to the human experience more broadly.

Having a central theme in your memoir is important because it gives your readers something to hold onto. It's what makes your story resonate with others, what makes it relatable, and what makes it memorable. Your central theme is what connects your story to the larger world, and what makes it more than just a collection of anecdotes and memories.

So, if you're thinking about writing a memoir, take the time to find your central theme. It may take some digging, some soul-searching, and maybe even a few tears, but it's worth it. Your central theme is what will give your memoir focus, depth, and meaning. It's what will make your story sing, and what will make it unforgettable.

How to find your unique focus

So, you're ready to find your central theme, huh? Let's get to it!

First things first: finding your central theme is like trying to find a needle in a haystack, or a matching sock in the dryer. It's not always easy, but it's definitely worth it. Your central theme is what will give your memoir focus, depth, and meaning. It's what will make your story sing, and what will make it unforgettable.

So, how do you find your central theme? Well, here are a few tips to get you started:

Think about what makes your story unique. What sets you apart from everyone else? What are the defining moments or experiences that have shaped you into the person you are today? What makes your story different from every other story out there?

Consider your passions and interests. What are the things that make you light up? What are the topics or themes that you're most drawn to? What are the things that you could talk about for hours on end?

Reflect on the emotions that come up when you think about your life experiences. What are the feelings that you associate with different moments in your life?

What are the things that make you feel most alive, most fulfilled, most joyful?

Look for patterns in your life experiences. What are the recurring themes or motifs that you see in your life story? What are the things that keep showing up, over and over again? What are the things that seem to be guiding you towards a particular path or direction?

Consider your audience. Who are you writing your memoir for? What are the things that they will be most interested in, most moved by, most inspired by? What are the things that will resonate with them on a deep, emotional level?

Explore different angles and perspectives. Sometimes, our central theme isn't immediately obvious. It may require looking at our life experiences from a different angle or perspective. Try approaching your story from different angles, like your relationships, your career, or your personal growth. You may be surprised at what you discover.

Don't be afraid to get vulnerable. Finding your central theme may require digging deep and getting uncomfortable. It may require confronting difficult emotions, painful memories, or uncomfortable truths. But remember, it's through our vulnerabilities that we connect with others on a deeper level. Your central theme may be something that you've been hiding or avoiding but embracing it may be the key to unlocking your story's true potential.

Sometimes, finding our central theme requires experimenting with different writing styles and formats. Maybe your story is best told through poetry, or through letters to your younger self, or through vignettes. Don't be afraid to play around with different styles and formats until you find the one that best captures your central theme.

Get feedback from others. Sometimes, we're too close to our own story to see the forest for the trees. Getting feedback from others can be a great way to gain fresh perspective and to identify the central themes and motifs that we may have missed. Find a trusted friend, family member, or writing group to share your work with, and ask for their honest feedback.

Remember, finding your central theme takes time and patience. It may require some soul searching, journaling, and maybe even a few glasses of wine. But don't worry, you've got this! Your central theme is out there, waiting for you to discover it. Just keep exploring, keep reflecting, and keep digging deeper. You never know what you might find.

Brainstorming techniques

So, you're ready to start brainstorming for your memoir, huh? Let's get to it!

First things first: brainstorming is like a treasure hunt. You're on a mission to uncover the gems, the hidden treasures, the nuggets of gold that will make your memoir shine. It's a process of exploration, of discovery, and of uncovering the unexpected.

Now, let's talk about some brainstorming techniques that can help you on your journey:

1. **Freewriting:** This technique involves setting a timer for a certain amount of time (say, 10 or 15 minutes), and then writing whatever comes to mind without stopping or editing. The goal is to keep the pen moving, even if it means writing nonsense or stream-of-consciousness thoughts. The idea is to bypass your inner critic and allow your thoughts and ideas to flow freely.

2. **Mind mapping:** This technique involves starting with a central idea or theme (like "childhood memories" or "career milestones"), and then branching out into sub-themes and related ideas. The goal is to create a visual representation of your ideas, and to see

the connections and relationships between different aspects of your life story.

3. **Listing:** This technique involves creating a list of ideas, memories, or themes related to your memoir. The goal is to generate as many ideas as possible, without worrying about their order or organization. The idea is to get everything down on paper, and then to sort through it later.

4. **Interviewing:** This technique involves interviewing yourself or others about your life experiences. The goal is to ask open-ended questions that encourage reflection and exploration, and to use the responses as a starting point for your memoir.

5. **Visual prompts:** This technique involves using visual prompts (like photographs, artwork, or objects) as a starting point for your memoir. The goal is to use the visuals as a jumping-off point for your memories and ideas, and to explore the connections and relationships between them.

6. **Use prompts:** Sometimes, it can be helpful to have a specific prompt to guide your brainstorming. You might choose a prompt like "the moment that changed everything," "the biggest risk I ever took," or "the people who shaped me." Use the prompt as a starting

point for your brainstorming and see where it takes you.

7. **Collaborate with others:** Brainstorming with others can be a great way to generate new ideas and perspectives. Find a writing partner, join a writing group, or collaborate with a friend or family member to bounce ideas off of each other and see where your combined creativity takes you.

8. **Take breaks:** Sometimes, stepping away from your brainstorming can be just as productive as diving in. Take breaks as needed to give your mind a chance to rest and recharge. Go for a walk, take a nap, or do something else that helps you relax and clear your mind. You might be surprised at the new ideas that come to you when you return to your brainstorming later.

9. **Keep an open mind:** Finally, remember that the most important part of brainstorming is keeping an open mind. Don't judge or censor your ideas as they come to you. Embrace the unexpected, the weird, and the surprising. You
never know what might turn out to be the gem that unlocks your memoir's potential.

Remember, the key to successful brainstorming is to keep an open mind and to embrace the unexpected.

Don't be afraid to explore new ideas, to try new techniques, and to push beyond your comfort zone. Your memoir is waiting to be written, and your brainstorming journey is just the beginning. So, get out there, have fun, and let your creativity soar!

Top 10 Popular Memoir Themes

Are you curious about the most popular themes in memoir writing? Let me tell you, these themes are like the seasoning that makes a good meal great. They add depth, emotion, and resonance to your story. So, without further ado, here are the top ten popular memoir themes:

1. **Coming of age:** This theme explores the experiences of growing up and transitioning into adulthood. It can include themes like self-discovery, identity formation, and the challenges of adolescence.

2. **Family relationships:** This theme explores the complex dynamics of family relationships, including themes like love, loss, conflict, and reconciliation. It can include stories of family dysfunction, estrangement, and reconciliation.

3. **Overcoming adversity:** This theme explores the experiences of overcoming obstacles and adversity, including themes like resilience, perseverance, and personal growth. It can include stories of illness, trauma, addiction, or overcoming other significant challenges.

4. **Career and professional development:** This theme explores the experiences of pursuing a career or professional passion, including themes like ambition, perseverance, and self-discovery. It can include stories of success, failure, and personal growth.

5. **Love and relationships:** This theme explores the complexities of romantic relationships, including themes like intimacy, commitment, and the challenges of love. It can include stories of dating, marriage, divorce, and everything in between.

6. **Travel and adventure:** This theme explores the experiences of traveling and exploring the world, including themes like discovery, culture shock, and personal growth. It can include stories of backpacking, exploring new cultures, and getting out of your comfort zone.

7. **Spiritual exploration:** This theme explores the experiences of spiritual exploration and growth, including themes like faith, doubt, and personal transformation. It can include stories of religious conversion, spiritual awakening, or finding meaning and purpose in life.

8. **Social justice and activism:** This theme explores the experiences of social justice and activism, including themes like advocacy, resistance, and personal empowerment. It can include stories of fighting for justice, standing up to oppression, and making a difference in the world.

9. **Creative expression:** This theme explores the experiences of creative expression, including themes like art, music, and writing. It can include stories of finding your creative voice, pursuing your artistic passions, and the joys and challenges of creative expression.

10. **Humor and satire:** This theme explores the experiences of using humor and satire to explore the absurdities of life, including themes like irony, sarcasm, and wit. It can include stories of finding the humor in difficult situations, using humor to cope with adversity, and poking fun at the quirks of human nature.

So, there you have it! The top ten popular themes in memoir writing. Remember, the most important thing is to find the theme that resonates with you and your story. It's your life, your story, and your unique perspective that will make your memoir shine. So, get out there, explore, and tell your story with heart and passion!

Crafting a Compelling Narrative

Establishing a narrative structure

The next step after finding your theme and focus is to establish your memoir's narrative structure. If you're ready, let's do this thing!

First things first: establishing a narrative structure is like building a house. You need a strong foundation, a solid framework, and a clear sense of purpose. It's what gives your memoir shape, direction, and meaning.

So, how do you establish a narrative structure? That's the question. Here are a few tips to get you started:

1. **Start with a clear goal:** What is the story you want to tell? What is the central message or theme that you want to convey? Having a clear goal in mind will help you establish a structure that supports your narrative and guides your readers.

2. **Map out the key moments:** What are the key moments or turning points in your story? What are the events that shaped you into the person you are today? Mapping out these moments will help you create a clear

narrative arc and establish a structure that supports your story.

3. **Choose a structure that works for you:** There are many different narrative structures to choose from, including chronological, thematic, and hybrid structures. Choose the one that works best for your story and your personal style.

4. **Use a hook to draw in your readers:** Your memoir should start with a hook that draws in your readers and sets the stage for your story. This could be an interesting anecdote, a powerful quote, or a striking image that captures the essence of your memoir.

5. **Consider the pacing:** Pacing is important in memoir writing. You want to create a structure that keeps your readers engaged and interested, while also allowing for moments of reflection and introspection. Experiment with different pacing techniques, like alternating between fast-paced action and slower, more reflective moments.

6. **Use transitions to guide your readers:** Transitions are important in establishing a narrative structure. They help guide your readers from one moment to the next and establish a sense of continuity and flow. Use transitions like scene breaks, chapter

breaks, and summary statements to keep your readers engaged and on track.

Remember, establishing a narrative structure takes time and effort. It may require some experimentation, some trial and error, and maybe even some swearing. But don't worry, you've got this! Your memoir is waiting to be written, and your narrative structure is the framework that will bring it to life. So, get out there, have fun, and let your creativity soar!

Showing vs. Telling

Are you ready to learn about the difference between showing and telling in memoir writing? Let's dive in!

First things first: showing versus telling is like the difference between watching a movie and reading a book report. Showing allows your readers to experience the story firsthand, to feel the emotions, and to connect with your experiences on a deeper level. Telling, on the other hand, can feel distant and detached, like a summary of events rather than a true story.

So, how do you show versus tell in your memoir writing? Here are a few tips to get you started:

1. **Use sensory details:** When you're showing in your writing, it's important to use sensory details to help your readers experience the scene. Use descriptive language to paint a picture of the setting, the characters, and the emotions of the moment. Use all five senses to create a vivid, immersive experience for your readers.

2. **Use dialogue:** Dialogue is a powerful tool for showing in your writing. It allows your characters to come alive on the page, and helps your readers connect

with them on a deeper level. Use dialogue to reveal character, advance the plot, and convey emotions.

3. **Show, don't tell:** This may seem obvious, but it's important to remember that showing is always more powerful than telling. Instead of telling your readers how you felt, show them through your actions, body language, and dialogue. Show them through vivid descriptions and sensory details.

4. **Use action:** Action is a powerful way to show your readers what's happening in your story. Use action to convey emotion, advance the plot, and reveal character. Instead of telling your readers how you felt, show them through your actions and reactions to the events unfolding around you.

5. **Be specific:** This is key when it comes to showing versus telling. Use specific details and examples to bring your story to life, and to help your readers connect with your experiences on a deeper level.

6. **Use body language:** Body language is a powerful way to show your readers what's happening in your story. Use body language to convey emotion, reveal character, and create tension. Instead of telling your readers how you felt, show them through your body language and the body language of those around you.

7. **Use metaphor and simile:** Metaphor and simile are powerful tools for showing in your writing. They allow you to create comparisons that bring your story to life and help your readers connect with your experiences on a deeper level. If you ever get confused, a quick refresher search is handy. Metaphors tend to use the words "are" or "is" like "She's a demon!" Similes tend to use words like "as" or "like," for example, "She's sweet as sugar." Either way, using these descriptives allows your reader to use their own imagination to visualize what they want to see without you describing every inch of something.

8. **Use descriptive verbs:** Descriptive verbs are another powerful tool for showing in your writing. Instead of using bland, generic verbs like "walked" or "talked," use more descriptive verbs that convey action and emotion. Try, based on the scenario, "glided" or "dashed." Each descriptive word you provide the reader ensures they are able to fully engage with your story.

9. **Use internal monologue:** Interior monologue is a powerful way to show your readers what's happening inside your head. Use internal monologue to reveal your thoughts, fears, and desires, and to help your readers connect with your experiences on a deeper level.

10. **Edit ruthlessly:** Finally, remember that showing versus telling is something that can be improved with careful editing. Take the time to go back through your writing and identify places where you're telling instead of showing. Then, make the necessary changes to bring those moments to life and create a more immersive experience for your readers.

Remember, showing versus telling is all about bringing your story to life and allowing your readers to experience it firsthand. It's about creating a vivid, immersive experience that leaves a lasting impact. So, get out there, have fun, and let your creativity soar!

Utilizing the Hero's Journey

Are you ready to learn about the hero's journey and how to use it to create a powerful narrative for your memoir? Let's go on an adventure!

First things first: the hero's journey is a classic storytelling structure that has been used for centuries to create powerful narratives. It's the blueprint for stories like Harry Potter, The Lord of the Rings, and Star Wars. And it can be used to create a powerful narrative for your memoir.

So, what is the hero's journey, and how can you use it to create your narrative? Here are a few tips to get you started:

1. **The call to adventure:** The hero's journey begins with a call to adventure, a moment that sets the story in motion. In your memoir, this could be a moment of crisis, a personal challenge, or a turning point in your life.

2. **Refusal of the call:** Next, the hero often hesitates before embarking on the journey, questioning their ability to succeed. In your memoir, this could be a moment of self-doubt or uncertainty, where you question your ability to overcome the challenges ahead.

3. **Meeting the mentor:** Every hero needs a mentor, someone who can guide them and provide them with the tools they need to succeed. In your memoir, this could be a person who inspires you, a teacher who helps you grow, or a mentor who guides you along the way.

4. **Crossing the threshold:** This is the moment when the hero leaves their ordinary world and enters the unknown. In your memoir, this could be a moment when you leave your comfort zone, take a risk, or step outside of your routine.

5. **Trials and tribulations:** Every hero faces challenges along the way, obstacles that they must overcome in order to succeed. In your memoir, these challenges could be personal struggles, external obstacles, or moments of crisis.

6. **The innermost cave:** This is the moment when the hero faces their greatest challenge, their darkest fear, or their biggest obstacle. In your memoir, this could be a moment of self-discovery, a personal revelation, or a moment of profound change.

7. **The resurrection:** This is the moment when the hero rises from the ashes, stronger and more determined than ever before. In your memoir, this

could be a moment of personal growth or a moment of triumph.

8. **The return home:** Finally, the hero returns home, transformed by their journey and ready to share their story with the world. In your memoir, this could be a moment of reflection, a moment of gratitude, or a moment of personal growth.

9. **Identify your hero's journey:** The hero's journey is not a one-size-fits-all structure. It's important to identify the unique aspects of your own journey and use them to create a narrative that is authentic and true to your experiences.

10. **Use archetypes to create relatable characters:** Archetypes, or universal symbols and patterns, can help you create relatable characters that resonate with your readers. Use archetypes like the mentor, the shadow, and the trickster to add depth and complexity to your story.

11. **Show, don't tell:** As we discussed earlier, showing versus telling is a powerful tool for creating an immersive experience for your readers. Use sensory details, dialogue, and descriptive language to show your readers the key moments of your hero's journey.

12. **Embrace vulnerability:** The hero's journey is not always easy, and it often requires a level of vulnerability and honesty that can be uncomfortable. But, it's these moments that create the most powerful and relatable narratives. Don't be afraid to share your struggles, your fears, and your failures along the way.

13. **Reflect on the journey:** Finally, take the time to reflect on your hero's journey and the lessons you've learned along the way. What insights have you gained? What have you learned about yourself, about others, and about the world? Use these reflections to create a powerful and meaningful ending to your memoir.

Remember, the hero's journey is a powerful tool for creating a narrative that resonates with your readers and inspires them to take action. But, it's the authenticity and honesty of your experiences that will truly bring your story to life. The most important part of the hero's journey is the journey itself, the moments of growth, change, and transformation that shape us into the people we are today. So, get out there, have fun, and let your creativity soar!

Top 10 Storytelling Techniques for Memoirs

Are you ready to learn about the top 10 storytelling techniques for memoirs? Let's get started!

1. **Show, don't tell:** As we discussed earlier, showing versus telling is a powerful tool for creating an immersive experience for your readers. Use sensory details, dialogue, and descriptive language to show your readers the key moments of your story.

2. **Use dialogue:** Dialogue is a powerful tool for bringing your characters to life and adding depth to your story. Use it to reveal character, advance the plot, and convey emotions.

3. **Use descriptive language:** Descriptive language is another powerful tool for creating an immersive experience for your readers. Use it to paint a vivid picture of the setting, the characters, and the emotions of the moment.

4. **Use flashbacks:** Flashbacks can be a powerful way to reveal backstory and add depth to your story. Use them sparingly, but effectively, to provide context and deepen your readers' understanding of your experiences.

5. **Use metaphor and simile:** Metaphor and simile are powerful tools for creating comparisons that bring your story to life and help your readers connect with your experiences on a deeper level.

6. **Use suspense:** Suspense is a powerful way to keep your readers engaged and interested in your story. Use it to create tension, build anticipation, and keep your readers on the edge of their seats.

7. **Use humor:** Humor can be a powerful tool for breaking up tension and adding levity to your story. Use it to show your readers that you don't take yourself too seriously, and to add a touch of humanity to your experiences.

8. **Use repetition:** Repetition can be a powerful way to reinforce key themes and ideas in your story. Use it to create a sense of continuity and to emphasize the importance of certain moments or experiences.

9. **Use sensory details:** Sensory details, like sight, sound, smell, taste, and touch, can be a powerful way to create a vivid, immersive experience for your readers. Use them to bring your story to life and engage your readers' senses.

10. **Use symbolism:** Symbolism is a powerful tool for creating meaning and adding depth to your story. Use it to represent ideas, emotions, and themes, and to connect with your readers on a deeper level.

Remember, storytelling is all about engaging your readers' emotions, connecting with their experiences, and creating a narrative that leaves a lasting impact. So, get out there, have fun, and let your creativity soar!

Developing Authentic Characters

Writing about yourself as a character

Are you ready to learn how to write about yourself as a character in your memoir? Let's dive in!

First things first: writing about yourself as a character is all about creating a three-dimensional portrait of yourself on the page. It's about showing your readers who you are, what you stand for, and what makes you unique. Here are a few tips to get you started:

1. **Embrace vulnerability:** As we discussed earlier, vulnerability is key to creating a powerful narrative. Don't be afraid to share your struggles, your fears, and your failures along the way. It's these moments of vulnerability that make your story relatable and compelling.

2. **Create a character arc:** Just like in a novel or a movie, your character in your memoir should have a clear arc, and by arc, I mean a journey that leads to personal growth and change. Identify the key moments in your journey, the challenges you faced, and the lessons you learned along the way.

3. **Use descriptive language:** Use descriptive language to paint a vivid picture of yourself on the page. Use sensory details, dialogue, and metaphor to show your readers who you are, rather than just telling them.

4. **Develop your character traits:** Just like in a novel, your character in your memoir should have distinct character traits that make them unique. Identify your strengths, your weaknesses, and the quirks that make you who you are.

5. **Use internal monologue:** Use internal monologue to reveal your thoughts, fears, and desires, and to help your readers connect with your experiences on a deeper level.

6. **Show, don't tell:** As we've discussed before, showing versus telling is a powerful tool for creating an immersive experience for your readers. Use sensory details, dialogue, and descriptive language to show your readers who you are, rather than just telling them.

7. **Use humor:** Humor can be a powerful tool for breaking up tension and adding levity to your story. Use it to show your readers that you don't take yourself too seriously, and to add a touch of humanity to your experiences.

8. **Use dialogue:** Dialogue is a powerful tool for bringing your character to life and adding depth to your story. Use it to reveal your character, advance the plot, and convey emotions.

9. **Use conflict:** Conflict is a crucial component of any story, and your memoir is no exception. Use the conflicts you faced on your journey to create tension, build anticipation, and keep your readers engaged.

10. **Use symbolism:** Symbolism is a powerful tool for creating meaning and adding depth to your story. Use it to represent ideas, emotions, and themes, and to connect with your readers on a deeper level.

11. **Show your flaws:** Don't be afraid to show your flaws and vulnerabilities in your character. It's these imperfections that make you relatable and human, and that allow your readers to connect with your story on a deeper level.

12. **Use flashbacks:** Flashbacks can be a powerful way to reveal backstory and add depth to your story. Use them to provide context and deepen your readers' understanding of your experiences.

13. **Be honest:** Finally, remember that honesty is the foundation of any good memoir. Don't sugarcoat your

experiences or try to paint yourself in a better light than you deserve. Your readers will appreciate your honesty and your willingness to be vulnerable.

Remember, writing about yourself as a character is all about creating a portrait of yourself that is authentic, relatable, and compelling. So, get out there, have fun, and let your creativity soar!

Describing Other People in Your Life

Are you ready to learn how to describe other people in your life in your memoir? Let's get started!

First things first: when writing about other people in your life, it's important to be respectful, honest, and fair. Here are a few tips to help you describe other people in your life in your memoir:

1. **Show, don't tell:** As we've discussed before, showing versus telling is a powerful tool for creating an immersive experience for your readers. Use sensory details, dialogue, and descriptive language to show your readers who the people in your life are, rather than just telling them.

2. **Use descriptive language:** Use descriptive language to paint a vivid picture of the people in your life on the page. Use sensory details, dialogue, and metaphor to show your readers who they are, rather than just telling them.

3. **Be respectful:** Remember that the people in your life are real people with their own feelings, emotions, and experiences. Be respectful of their privacy and

their feelings and avoid sharing anything that could be hurtful or damaging.

4. **Be honest:** That being said, honesty is also important when writing about other people in your life. Don't sugarcoat their flaws or exaggerate their strengths. Instead, be honest and fair in your portrayal of them.

5. **Show their impact on your life:** The people in your life have had a significant impact on who you are today. Use your memoir to explore those relationships and to show your readers how they've influenced your journey.

6. **Use dialogue:** Dialogue is a powerful tool for bringing the people in your life to life on the page. Use it to reveal their character, advance the plot, and convey their emotions.

7. **Use flashbacks:** Flashbacks can be a powerful way to reveal backstory and add depth to your story. Use them to provide context and deepen your readers' understanding of the people in your life.

8. **Use humor:** Humor can be a powerful tool for adding levity to your story and showing the people in your life in a more relatable light. Use it to add a touch of humanity to your experiences.

Remember, writing about the people in your life is all about creating a portrait of them that is respectful, honest, and fair. So, get out there, have fun, and let your creativity soar!

Balancing Honesty and Compassion

Are you ready to learn how to balance honesty and compassion in your personal memoir? If so, let's dive in! First things first: writing a personal memoir can be a delicate balancing act. On one hand, you want to be honest and authentic about your experiences. On the other hand, you don't want to hurt the people you care about or damage their reputations. Here are a few tips to help you find the right balance:

1. **Be honest:** Honesty is the foundation of any good memoir. Don't sugarcoat your experiences or try to make yourself look better than you are. Be honest about your struggles, your flaws, and your mistakes.

2. **Use compassion:** Remember that the people in your life are real people with their own feelings, emotions, and experiences. Use compassion to show them in a more understanding light, and to avoid sharing anything that could be hurtful or damaging.

3. **Show empathy:** Empathy is the ability to understand and share the feelings of another person. Use it to show your readers that you understand the people in your life and the impact that they've had on your journey.

4. **Be respectful:** Remember to be respectful of the people in your life and their privacy. Avoid sharing anything that could be hurtful or damaging and ask for their permission before sharing any personal details about them.

5. **Use discretion:** Use discretion when sharing personal details about the people in your life. Ask yourself if it's necessary to share certain details, and if it could potentially harm anyone's reputation or relationships.

6. **Use sensitivity:** Use sensitivity to show the people in your life in a more positive light. Highlight their strengths and positive qualities and avoid dwelling on their flaws or negative qualities.

7. **Use humor:** Humor can be a powerful tool for adding levity to your story and showing the people in your life in a more relatable light. Use it to add a touch of humanity to your experiences and to show that you don't take yourself too seriously.

Remember, balancing honesty and compassion is all about finding the right balance between authenticity and empathy. So, get out there, have fun, and let your creativity soar!

Top 10 Tips for Creating Memorable Characters

Are you ready to learn the top ten tips for creating memorable characters in your writing? Let's get started!

2. **Give them unique traits:** Memorable characters often have unique traits or quirks that make them stand out from the crowd. Think about the people in your life and the things that make them unique and try to incorporate those traits into your characters.

3. **Make them relatable:** Relatable characters are more memorable because readers can see themselves in them. Give your characters flaws and challenges that your readers can identify with.

4. **Create strong motivations:** Every memorable character has a strong motivation that drives them forward. Whether it's a desire for revenge, love, or power, make sure your characters have clear motivations that make sense for their actions.

5. **Give them conflicts:** Characters with conflicts are more interesting because they have something

at stake. Give your characters conflicts that challenge them and force them to grow.

6. **Make them dynamic:** Dynamic characters change and grow throughout the course of your story. Give your characters a character arc that shows how they've grown and changed over time.

7. **Use descriptive language:** Use descriptive language to paint a vivid picture of your characters. Use sensory details, dialogue, and metaphor to show your readers who they are, rather than just telling them.

8. **Show their flaws:** Flawed characters are more interesting because they feel more human. Don't be afraid to show your characters' flaws and vulnerabilities.

9. **Use humor:** Humor can be a powerful tool for creating memorable characters. Use it to add levity to your story and to show your characters in a more relatable and human light.

10. **Give them backstories:** Every character has a backstory that informs who they are and why they act the way they do. Create rich backstories for your characters that help your readers understand who they are.

11. **Make them unique:** Finally, make sure your characters are unique and stand out from other characters in your story. Give them distinct personalities and voices that make them memorable.

Remember, creating memorable characters is all about giving them unique traits, making them relatable, and giving them strong motivations and conflicts. So, get out there, have fun, and let your creativity soar!

Setting the Scene: Writing Descriptive Settings and Context

Importance of Setting

Are you ready to learn about the importance of the setting in a memoir story? If so, let's get started!

The setting of your memoir story is like the backdrop of a painting. It's the context that surrounds your experiences, and it helps to create a more immersive and vivid experience for your readers. Here are a few reasons why setting is so important:

1. **It creates a sense of place:** It can transport them to another time and place and help them to feel like they're right there with you.

2. **It adds depth and richness to your story:** It can help to set the mood and tone of your story and add layers of meaning and symbolism.

3. **It sets the stage for your experiences:** It can help your readers understand the context and background of your story and provide important context for your experiences.

4. **It creates a sense of nostalgia:** It can transport them back to a different time and place and help them to remember their own experiences from that time.

5. **It can reflect your internal landscape:** It can help to convey your emotions and feelings and add a deeper layer of meaning to your story.

6. **It can create tension and conflict:** For example, if your story takes place in a turbulent or dangerous environment, this can create a sense of danger and uncertainty for your readers.

7. **It can create a sense of time and history:** It can help to anchor your story in a particular era or time period and provide important context for your experiences.

8. **It can be a character in itself:** In some cases, the setting can be a character in itself. It can have its own personality and quirks and add an extra layer of depth and meaning to your story.

9. **It can help to create a mood:** For example, if your story takes place in a dark and foreboding forest, this can create a sense of tension and suspense for your readers.

10. **It can inspire creativity:** Finally, the setting can inspire creativity in your writing. It can spark your imagination and help you to come up with new ideas and perspectives for your story.

Remember, the setting is an important part of your memoir story. It can add depth and richness to your experiences and create a more immersive and vivid experience for your readers. So, get out there, have fun, and let your creativity soar!

Writing Vivid Descriptions

Are you ready to learn about the importance of writing vivid descriptions? If so, let's dive in!

Vivid descriptions are like a spice rack for your writing. They add flavor, color, and depth to your story, and help to create a more immersive and engaging experience for your readers. Here are a few reasons why writing vivid descriptions is so important:

1. **It creates a sense of place:** It can transport them to another time and place and help them to feel like they're right there with you.

2. **It adds depth and richness to your story:** It can help to set the mood and tone of your story and add layers of meaning and symbolism.

3. **It engages the senses:** It can help them to see, hear, smell, taste, and feel your experiences in a more immersive way.

4. **It makes your writing more interesting:** It helps to capture the attention of your readers and keep them hooked on your story.

5. It helps your readers to visualize your story: It can help them to create a mental image of your experiences and feel like they're right there with you.

6. It can convey emotions and feelings: For example, if you describe the sound of rain as a soothing lullaby, this can help your readers understand the calming effect rain has on you.

7. It creates a memorable experience: If you describe a beautiful sunset in a way that makes your readers feel like they're watching it with you, they're more likely to remember that experience.

8. It helps to create a unique voice: The way you describe things can be a reflection of your personality and style, and help your readers connect with you on a deeper level.

9. It adds authenticity to your story: By describing things in some detail, you can make your experiences feel more real and relatable to your readers.

10. It can be fun and enjoyable: Finally, it allows you to play with language and creativity and express yourself in unique and interesting ways.

Using Historical Context Effectively

Are you ready to learn about the importance of using historical context effectively when writing a memoir? If so, let's get started!

Using historical context effectively in your memoir is like seasoning a dish with the perfect blend of spices. We added some salt and pepper with the vivid words, but now you're gonna add some cayenne or garlic to really bring the flavor home! It adds depth and richness to your story, and helps your readers understand the cultural, social, and political forces that shaped your experiences. Here are a few reasons why using historical context is so important:

1. **It provides important context:** It helps your readers understand the events and experiences that shaped your life and provides a broader perspective on your experiences.

2. **It adds depth and richness to your story:** It can help you to explore the cultural, social, and political forces that shaped your experiences, and add layers of meaning and symbolism to your story.

3. It creates a sense of nostalgia: It can transport them back to a different time and place and help them to remember their own experiences from that time.

4. It creates a sense of time and history: It can help to anchor your story in a particular era or time period and provide important context for your experiences.

5. It helps your readers understand your experiences: It can help them to see how the events and forces of the time impacted your life and create a deeper connection with your story.

6. It adds authenticity to your story: By incorporating historical details, you can make your experiences feel more real and relatable to your readers.

7. It can highlight social issues: Historical context can also highlight important social issues that were prevalent during the time period of your memoir. This can help to add depth and meaning to your story and make it more impactful.

8. It can create a more engaging experience: It can help to bring your story to life and create a vivid, immersive experience that your readers won't forget.

9. **It can inspire curiosity:** It may encourage them to learn more about the time period and the events that shaped your experiences and inspire them to read more about history in general.

10. **It can make your story more universal:** Finally, using historical context can make your story more universal. It can help your readers see how your experiences are connected to broader historical trends and make your story relevant to a wider audience.

Remember, using historical context effectively is an important part of creating a compelling and meaningful memoir. So, get out there, have fun, and let your creativity soar!

Top 10 Techniques for Writing About Place and Time

Are you ready to learn about the top ten techniques for writing about a place and time in a memoir? If so, let's get started!

Writing about a place and time in your memoir is like painting a picture with words. It allows your readers to see, hear, smell, taste, and feel your experiences in a more immersive and vivid way. Here are a few techniques you can use to bring your setting to life:

1. **Use sensory details:** Use sensory details to help your readers experience the place and time you're writing about. Describe the sights, sounds, smells, tastes, and textures of the environment in detail to create a more immersive experience.

2. **Describe the culture and social norms:** Describe the culture and social norms of the place and time you're writing about. This can help your readers understand the context of your experiences and create a more authentic and nuanced portrayal of the setting.

3. **Incorporate historical events:** Incorporate historical events into your writing to add depth and richness to your story. This can help your readers

understand the broader social and political context of the time period, and make your experiences feel more relevant and impactful.

4. **Use dialogue:** Use dialogue to create a more engaging and dynamic portrayal of the place and time you're writing about. This can help your readers understand the nuances of the language and social interactions of the time period.

5. **Show, don't tell:** Show your readers what the place and time you're writing about was like, rather than simply telling them. Use vivid and descriptive language to paint a picture of the setting and bring it to life.

6. **Use metaphors and symbolism:** Use metaphors and symbolism to add depth and meaning to your writing. This can help your readers understand the emotional and psychological impact of the setting on your experiences.

7. **Use humor:** Use humor to create a more engaging and relatable portrayal of the place and time you're writing about. This can help your readers connect with your experiences on a more personal level.

8. **Use research:** Use research to ensure the accuracy and authenticity of your portrayal of the place and time you're writing about. Don't rely only on your memories.

This can help to create a more nuanced and realistic portrayal of the setting.

9. **Use contrast:** Use contrast to create a more dynamic and interesting portrayal of the place and time you're writing about. This can help your readers understand the differences and similarities between your experiences and the broader social and cultural context.

10. **Use your personal experiences:** Finally, use your personal experiences to create a unique and meaningful portrayal of the place and time you're writing about. This can help your readers connect with your story on a deeper level and create a more memorable reading experience.

Remember, writing about a place and time in your memoir is an important part of bringing your experiences to life. By using these techniques, you can create a more immersive and engaging portrayal of the setting, and help your readers connect with your story on a deeper level. So, get out there, have fun, and let your creativity soar!

Finding Your Voice and Style

Defining Your Writing Style

Are you ready to learn about the importance of defining your personal writing style? Let's get started!

Defining your personal writing style is like finding your signature scent. It sets you apart from others and helps you create a unique and memorable reading experience for your audience. Here are a few reasons why defining your personal writing style is so important:

1. **It sets you apart:** Defining your personal writing style sets you apart from other writers. It helps you stand out in a crowded market and creates a more memorable reading experience for your audience.

2. **It reflects your personality:** Your personal writing style reflects your personality and individuality as a writer. It's a reflection of your unique voice, tone, and perspective, and can help your readers connect with you on a deeper level.

3. **It creates consistency:** Defining your personal writing style creates consistency in your writing. It helps you maintain a clear and cohesive voice throughout your work and creates a more polished and professional reading experience for your audience.

4. It helps you find your niche: Defining your personal writing style can help you find your niche as a writer. It can help you identify the types of stories and topics that you're passionate about and create a more focused and intentional approach to your writing.

5. It adds authenticity to your work: It helps you create a more honest and genuine portrayal of your experiences and creates a deeper connection with your audience.

6. It helps you develop your voice: By identifying the elements that make your writing unique, you can hone your craft and refine your skills over time.

7. It makes writing easier: When you've defined your personal writing style, writing actually becomes easier and more natural. It's almost conversational. You know what works for you and what doesn't, and you can focus on developing your strengths rather than struggling to imitate someone else's style.

8. It can attract a specific audience: Your personal writing style can truly attract a specific audience that resonates with your voice and perspective. By creating a unique and authentic portrayal of your experiences, you can connect with readers who share your interests and values. Some authors swear or crack jokes in their manuscripts while others are more proper and less casual. You do you. (You can probably tell; I'm one of the more casual writing styles.)

9. **It adds value to your work:** It creates a more cohesive and polished reading experience for your audience and adds a unique and memorable element to your writing.

10. **It helps you stay motivated:** Finally, defining your personal writing style can even help you stay motivated and inspired. By identifying the elements that make your writing unique and valuable, you can stay focused on your goals, continue to grow and develop as a writer, and actually enjoy your writing journey.

Remember, defining your personal writing style is an important part of creating a successful and engaging memoir. It helps you stand out in a crowded market, connect with your audience on a deeper level, and stay motivated and inspired throughout the writing process. So, get out there, have fun, and let your creativity soar!

The Role of Humor, Emotion, and Tone

Well, hello! Are you ready to learn about the importance of understanding the role of humor, emotion, and tone in writing a memoir? Let's get started!

Writing a memoir is like a rollercoaster ride of emotions. Incorporating humor, emotion, and tone can make the journey even more exciting. Here are a few reasons why understanding the role of humor, emotion, and tone is so important:

1. **Humor adds levity:** It can help to break up heavy or emotional topics and create a more engaging and relatable reading experience for your audience.

2. **Emotion creates connection:** When you share your personal experiences and emotions, it helps your readers connect with you on a deeper level and feel invested in your story.

3. **Tone sets the mood:** It can create a sense of nostalgia, anticipation, or reflection, depending on the tone you choose to use. The tone can also create a unique voice for your memoir that helps it stand out.

4. Humor can enhance the emotional impact: It can create contrast between the lighter and heavier moments and make the emotional moments even more powerful.

5. Emotion can make your story memorable: It can help your readers understand your experiences in a more profound way and create a lasting impact on their lives.

6. Tone can reflect the theme: For example, if your memoir is about overcoming adversity, a hopeful and resilient tone can reinforce this message and create a more impactful reading experience.

7. Humor can reveal character: It can show your readers your unique voice and perspective and make your story more relatable and engaging.

8. Emotion can inspire empathy: Sharing your emotions in your memoir can inspire empathy in your readers. It can help them understand your experiences in a more personal way and create a deeper emotional connection with your story.

9. Tone can create suspense: The tone of your memoir can create suspense and tension, especially if you're writing about a particularly dramatic or emotional event. It can keep your readers engaged and invested in your story, eager to see how it will unfold.

10. Humor and emotion can work together: Finally, using humor and emotion together can create a powerful and impactful reading experience. It can create a balance between lightness and seriousness and create a nuanced and authentic portrayal of your experiences.

Remember, incorporating humor, emotion, and tone into your memoir is an important part of creating a compelling and engaging story. By understanding the role of these elements, you can create a more memorable and impactful reading experience for your audience. So, get out there, have fun, and let your creativity soar!

Crafting Compelling Dialogue

Alrighty! Are you ready to learn about the importance of crafting compelling dialogue in writing a memoir? Let's get started!

Crafting compelling dialogue in your memoir is like bringing your story to life. It allows your readers to hear the voices of the people you interacted with and experience your conversations in a more immersive way. Here are a few reasons why crafting compelling dialogue is so important:

1. **Dialogue adds authenticity:** Including dialogue in your memoir adds authenticity to your story. It helps to create a more realistic portrayal of the people you interacted with and the conversations you had and makes your story more relatable to your readers.

2. **Dialogue creates drama:** Dialogue creates drama and tension in your memoir. It can help to break up heavy or emotional topics and create a more engaging and dynamic reading experience for your audience.

3. **Dialogue reveals character:** Dialogue reveals character and personality. It can show your readers the nuances of the people you interacted with and make your story more complex and nuanced.

4. **Dialogue adds variety:** It creates a break from descriptive passages and can make your story more dynamic and interesting to read.

5. **Dialogue can create humor:** It can show the wit and humor of the people you interact with and create a more lighthearted reading experience for your audience.

6. **Dialogue can convey information:** It can reveal details about the people you interacted with, their perspectives, and their motivations, and help your readers understand your experiences on a deeper level.

7. **Dialogue can create conflict:** This can add drama to your story and create a more engaging and dynamic reading experience for your audience.

8. **Dialogue can reveal cultural differences:** Dialogue can also reveal cultural differences and provide insight into the social and historical context of your memoir. It can show how people from different backgrounds and cultures interact and communicate and create a richer and more nuanced portrayal of your experiences.

9. **Dialogue can create intimacy:** Dialogue can create a sense of intimacy between the reader and the characters in your memoir. It can make your readers

feel like they're part of the conversation and create a more personal and emotional connection with your story.

10. **Dialogue can make your story memorable:** Finally, crafting compelling dialogue can make your story more memorable. It can create a unique and authentic portrayal of your experiences and the people you interacted with, and make your story stand out in a crowded market.

Remember, including dialogue in your memoir is an important part of creating a successful and engaging story. By understanding the importance of crafting compelling dialogue, you can create a more authentic, nuanced, and memorable portrayal of your experiences. So, get out there, have fun, and let your creativity soar!

Top 10 Tips for Finding Your Unique Voice

Okay! Are you ready to learn about the top ten tips for finding your unique voice when writing a memoir? Let's get started!

Finding your unique voice when writing a memoir is like finding your own personal style. It allows you to stand out from the crowd and create a more authentic and engaging reading experience for your audience. Here are a few tips to help you find your unique voice:

1. **Write like you talk:** Write in a way that's natural and authentic to you. Use your own voice and your own unique way of expressing yourself.

2. **Don't be afraid to be yourself:** Embrace your quirks and idiosyncrasies. Don't try to conform to what you think others want to read.

3. **Read widely:** Read memoirs by different authors to get a sense of what works and what doesn't. Pay attention to their writing style and how they express themselves.

4. **Practice writing every day:** The more you write, the easier it becomes to find your unique voice. Practice writing every day, even if it's just for a few minutes.

5. **Experiment with different writing styles:** Try writing in different styles to see what works best for you. You may find that a certain style comes more naturally to you than others.

6. **Focus on your strengths:** Identify your strengths as a writer and focus on developing them. This will help you create a unique and memorable reading experience for your audience.

7. **Write with purpose:** Identify the purpose of your memoir and write with that purpose in mind. This will help you create a more focused and cohesive narrative.

8. **Share your personal experiences:** Share your personal experiences and emotions in your writing. This will help you create a more authentic and relatable portrayal of your experiences.

9. **Edit ruthlessly:** Edit your writing ruthlessly to ensure that every word is intentional and necessary. This will help you refine your voice and make it more distinctive.

10. **Be patient:** Finding your unique voice takes time and practice. Be patient and keep writing, and you'll eventually find your own personal style.

Remember, finding your unique voice is an important part of creating a successful and engaging memoir. By following these tips, you can develop your writing style and create a more authentic and memorable reading experience for your audience. So, get out there, have fun, and let your creativity soar!

Overcoming Writer's Block and Staying Motivated

Common Reasons for Writer's Block

Hey! Hey! Hey! Are you struggling with writer's block? Don't worry, you're not alone! Let's take a look at the top ten reasons for writer's block and see if we can find a way to kick it to the curb.

1. **Fear of failure:** One of the biggest reasons for writer's block is fear of failure. You may be worried that your writing isn't good enough, or that you won't be able to live up to your own expectations.

2. **Perfectionism:** Similar to fear of failure, perfectionism can also lead to writer's block. You may feel like your writing needs to be perfect before you can move on, which can be paralyzing.

3. **Lack of inspiration:** Sometimes, you just don't know what to write about. Lack of inspiration can be a major roadblock for many writers. Find a writing community and throw ideas off each other to keep each other inspired.

4. Distractions: Distractions can also contribute to writer's block. It's hard to focus on your writing when your phone keeps buzzing, or your roommate won't stop talking or your belly is growling. Turn off the distractions before you sit down to write.

5. Procrastination: Procrastination is another common cause of writer's block. You may feel like you have all the time in the world to write and end up putting it off until the last minute. Hint: That's not good.

6. Burnout: Writing can be exhausting, and burnout is a real thing. If you're feeling burnt out, it can be hard to find the motivation to write. Take short breaks, call a friend, go to lunch, or go turn on some movie previews to refresh the activity in your brain.

7. Lack of structure: If you don't have a clear plan or structure for your writing, it can be difficult to get started. An outline is a must in my opinion. Others might disagree, but I suspect they finish fewer books.

8. Self-doubt: Self-doubt is another major contributor to writer's block. You may be questioning your abilities as a writer, or wondering if your writing is worth sharing with the world. Hint: It is. Tell the voice to hush and keep writing.

9. **Overthinking:** Sometimes, we can overthink things and make them more complicated than they need to be. This can lead to writer's block and prevent us from getting started. Again, if you have a plan or an outline, overthinking should go away.

10. **Comparisonitis:** Finally, comparisonitis is a common cause of writer's block. You may be comparing yourself to other writers and feeling like you don't measure up. Whatever you call it, this isn't healthy, and you deserve better. Be who you are and know that your story matters!

Remember, writer's block is a common challenge for many writers. By identifying the reasons behind your writer's block, you can take steps to overcome it and get back to writing. So, take a deep breath, and let's get those creative juices flowing again!

Strategies for Overcoming Writer's Block

It's almost inevitable that you're going to struggle with writer's block at some point. Don't worry, we've got you covered with the top ten strategies for overcoming writer's block! Let's dive.

1. **Write every day:** Writing every day can help you get into a routine and make it easier to get started. Even if you don't feel like writing, make yourself sit down and write something, anything!

2. **Take a break:** Sometimes, the best way to overcome writer's block is to take a break. Go for a walk, watch a movie, or take a nap. Give your brain a chance to recharge.

3. **Change your environment:** Changing your environment can help you get out of a rut. Go to a coffee shop, sit outside, or move to a different room.

4. **Write something else:** If you're stuck on one project, try writing something else. This can help you get the creative juices flowing and break through your writer's block.

5. **Set small goals:** Setting small goals can make writing feel less overwhelming. Break your writing into manageable chunks and focus on one thing at a time.

6. **Use prompts:** Writing prompts can be a great way to get started when you're feeling stuck. There are tons of writing prompts available online, so find one that inspires you and start writing!

7. **Freewrite:** Freewriting is a technique where you write without stopping for a set amount of time. This can help you get past your inner critic and write more freely.

8. **Talk it out:** Sometimes, talking to someone about your writing can help you get unstuck. Find a friend or writing group and bounce ideas off of them.

9. **Read:** Reading can help you get inspired and spark new ideas. Read a book in your genre or read something completely different to get your brain working in a different way.

10. **Give yourself permission to write badly:** Finally, give yourself permission to write badly. Sometimes, the fear of writing something terrible can be paralyzing. Remember, the first draft is just that – a draft. You can always revise and improve later.

Setting realistic goals

Let's do some straight talk. Do you have realistic goals? Sometimes people set the bar way too low because they don't have the confidence that they will crush the goals. Others set such lofty goals, they totally set themselves up for failure.

Are you ready to set some realistic goals for writing your memoir? Let's get started with the top ten strategies for setting realistic goals.

1. **Be specific:** The more specific you are about your goals, the easier it is to achieve them. Instead of saying "I want to write a memoir," set a specific goal, like "I want to write 500 words a day."

2. **Break it down:** Writing a memoir can feel overwhelming, so break it down into smaller, more manageable goals. Set goals for each chapter or section, rather than trying to write the entire book at once.

3. **Prioritize:** Make writing a priority by setting aside time each day or each week for writing. This will help you stay on track and make steady progress towards your goals.

4. Create a routine: Creating a routine can help you stay focused and make writing a habit. Find a time and place where you can write every day and stick to it.

5. Celebrate small successes: Celebrate your small successes along the way, like completing a chapter or hitting a word count goal. This will keep you motivated and help you stay on track.

6. Be realistic: Set realistic goals that are achievable within your timeframe. Don't try to write a whole book in a week – that's just setting yourself up for failure.

7. Give yourself breaks: Taking breaks is important for preventing burnout and staying motivated. Make sure to schedule some rest days or downtime to recharge.

8. Measure progress: Keep track of your progress by tracking your word count, page count, or other measurable goals. This will help you see how far you've come and stay motivated.

9. Get feedback: Getting feedback from others can help you stay motivated and make progress. Join a writing group, share your work with a friend, or hire a writing coach to give you feedback and support.

10. **Adjust your goals as needed:** Finally, be flexible and adjust your goals as needed. If you're not making progress or feeling overwhelmed, it's okay to adjust your goals or take a step back and reassess.

Remember, setting realistic goals is an important part of writing a successful memoir. By following these strategies, you can stay motivated, make progress, and achieve your writing goals. So, let's get to it – you've got this!

Top 10 Tips for Maintaining Motivation and Self-Discipline

Are you struggling to maintain motivation and self-discipline when writing your memoir? Don't worry, we've got you covered with the top ten strategies for staying motivated and disciplined. Let's do this!

1. **Set realistic goals:** Setting realistic goals is the first step towards maintaining motivation and self-discipline. Make sure your goals are achievable within your timeframe.

2. **Create a routine:** Creating a routine can help you stay on track and make writing a habit. Find a time and place where you can write every day and stick to it.

3. **Eliminate distractions:** Distractions can derail your writing efforts, so try to eliminate them as much as possible. Put your phone on silent, close your email, and find a quiet place to write.

4. **Hold yourself accountable:** Hold yourself accountable by setting deadlines and tracking your progress. This will help you stay motivated and on track.

5. **Take breaks:** Taking breaks is important for preventing burnout and maintaining motivation. Make sure to schedule some rest days or downtime to recharge.

6. **Find inspiration:** Finding inspiration can help you stay motivated and excited about your writing. Read books in your genre, listen to podcasts, or take a walk outside to get inspired.

7. **Join a writing group:** Joining a writing group can provide you with support, feedback, and accountability. Find a group online or in-person and share your work with others.

8. **Celebrate small successes:** Celebrate your small successes along the way, like completing a chapter or hitting a word count goal. This will keep you motivated and help you stay on track.

9. **Visualize success:** Visualize yourself achieving your writing goals and imagine how it will feel to finish your memoir. This can help you stay motivated and focused on your writing.

10. **Keep a positive mindset:** Maintaining a positive mindset is crucial for staying motivated and disciplined. Remember, writing a memoir is a journey, not a destination. Celebrate your successes and don't

be too hard on yourself when things don't go as planned.

Staying motivated and disciplined when writing a memoir can be challenging, but it's not impossible. By following these strategies, you can stay focused, motivated, and disciplined throughout the writing process. So, let's get to it – you've got this!

Editing and Revising Your Memoir

The Importance of Self-Editing

Are you wondering why self-editing is vital when writing a personal memoir? Don't worry, we've got you covered with the top ten reasons.

1. **Catching mistakes:** The first reason self-editing is vital is because it allows you to catch mistakes before they're published. Whether it's a typo, a grammatical error, or a factual mistake, self-editing can help you catch and correct it.

2. **Improving clarity:** By reading your work critically, you can identify areas where your writing might be confusing or unclear and make changes to improve it.

3. **Refining your voice:** By reading your work aloud and critically evaluating your word choice and phrasing, you can make sure your writing sounds like you.

4. **Ensuring consistency:** By checking for consistency in character names, plot points, and

timelines, you can make sure your memoir is coherent and easy to follow.

5. **Cutting unnecessary content:** By evaluating each sentence and paragraph critically, you can remove anything that doesn't contribute to the overall story.

6. **Streamlining your writing:** By tightening up your sentences and removing unnecessary words, you can make your writing more concise and impactful.

7. **Enhancing readability:** By breaking up long paragraphs, using subheadings, and incorporating white space, you can make your memoir easier to read and more engaging.

8. **Improving pacing:** By evaluating the flow of your story and making changes to the order of events, you can ensure that your memoir is engaging and well-paced.

9. **Polishing your writing:** Self-editing can also help you polish your writing to a high standard. By carefully evaluating each sentence and polishing your prose, you can make your memoir shine.

10. **Making it the best it can be:** Finally, self-editing is vital because it allows you to make your memoir the best it can be. By taking the time to carefully edit and

revise your work, you can ensure that your memoir is the best it can be before you share it with the world.

Remember, self-editing is a vital part of the writing process, especially when it comes to personal memoirs. By following these reasons and taking the time to carefully edit and revise your work, you can ensure that your memoir is the best it can be. So, let's get to it – you've got this!

Techniques for Revising Content and Structure

You may be wondering about revisions. It can be a bit intimidating, but don't worry, we've got you covered with the top ten techniques for revising.

1. **Take a break:** The first technique for revising is to take a break and put your memoir aside for a few days or even a week before revising. This will give you fresh eyes and a new perspective.

2. **Evaluate your structure:** The next technique is to look at the order of events and the pacing of your story. Consider rearranging or cutting content to improve the flow of your memoir.

3. **Cut unnecessary content:** Remove any scenes or details that don't move the story forward or contribute to the overall theme of your memoir.

4. **Refine your voice:** Make sure your writing sounds like you and that your personality shines through.

5. **Check for consistency:** Make sure your character names, settings, and timelines are consistent and that there are no plot holes.

6. Enhance descriptions: Use sensory details and vivid language to paint a picture for your readers.

7. Incorporate feedback: Incorporate feedback from beta readers or writing groups into your revisions. Consider their suggestions and make changes as needed.

8. Tighten up your writing: Tighten up your writing by removing unnecessary words or phrases. Make sure each sentence is clear and concise.

9. Use active voice: Use active voice instead of passive voice in your writing. This makes your writing more engaging and easier to read.

10. Read aloud: Finally, read your memoir aloud during the revision process. This will help you identify areas where your writing may be unclear or awkward.

Remember, revising your memoir is an important part of the writing process. By following these techniques and taking the time to carefully revise your work, you can ensure that your memoir is the best it can be. So, let's get to it – you've got this!

Proofreading and Polishing Your Work

Alrighty! Are you ready to proofread and polish your personal memoir? We've got you covered with the top ten methods.

1. **Print it out:** The first method is to print out your memoir. I'm actually not a fan of killing trees by printing unnecessarily, but many people find that reading a physical copy can help you catch mistakes that you might miss on a screen.

2. **Read it aloud:** This can help you catch errors and improve the flow of your writing.

3. **Use a spellchecker/proofreader:** Use a spellchecker to catch any spelling errors that you may have missed. I find that Microsoft Word's editor is almost as good as Grammarly Pro lately, and in some areas, even better. It may seem like overkill, but I tend to run my drafts through both Grammarly and Word. Just be aware that spellcheckers won't catch all errors, so you still need to proofread manually.

4. **Check for grammar errors:** Check for grammar errors manually. You can find grammar guides or online resources readily on the internet. Make sure your sentences are clear and correctly punctuated.

5. **Use a beta reader:** A beta reader can provide valuable feedback on your memoir, helping you catch errors and identify areas for improvement.

6. **Take a break:** Taking a break before proofreading can help you approach your work with fresh eyes. Give yourself some time away from your memoir before proofreading.

7. **Read in reverse:** Reading your memoir backwards, from end to beginning, can help you catch mistakes that you might miss when reading forwards. Typically, this is done sentence by sentence. It doesn't make sense story-wise, but that's exactly the point. Your eyes catch the errors, more than allowing your mind to follow the story.

8. **Refer to your outline:** Assuming you created an outline before you began your journey with your memoir, you should be making regular visits to ensure you're staying on track. If you alter your course, make sure you update the outline as well. In this final phase of polishing your memoir, you want to make sure that the journey was logical, engaging, and emotionally charged.

9. **Check for consistency:** Check for consistency in your memoir, including character names, settings, and

timelines. Make sure everything is accurate and consistent throughout your memoir.

10. **Hire a professional editor:** Finally, consider hiring a professional editor to polish your memoir. An editor can provide valuable feedback and catch errors that you may have missed.

Remember, proofreading and polishing your memoir is an important part of the writing process. By following these methods and taking the time to carefully proofread and polish your work, you can ensure that your memoir is the best it can be. So, let's get to it – you've got this!

Top 10 Editing Tips for Memoir Writers

It's time to edit your personal memoir! Don't worry, we've got you covered with the top ten editing tips and hacks.

1. **Use a checklist:** The first tip is to use a checklist when editing your memoir. This will help you stay organized and ensure that you don't miss anything.

2. **Eliminate filler words:** Eliminating filler words is an effective editing hack. Words like "just," "very," and "really" can often be removed without changing the meaning of your sentence.

3. **Vary your sentence structure:** Varying your sentence structure can improve the flow of your writing and keep your readers engaged. Try mixing up short and long sentences and using different sentence structures.

4. **Cut adverbs:** Cutting adverbs is another effective editing hack. Adverbs like "quickly" and "loudly" can often be replaced with stronger verbs.

5. **Use active voice:** Using active voice instead of passive voice can make your writing more engaging and easier to read.

6. Check for repetition: Check for repetition in your writing, including repeated phrases, words, or themes. This can make your writing feel monotonous or redundant.

7. Read your work aloud: Reading your work aloud is a helpful editing hack. This can help you identify awkward phrasing, unclear sentences, and other issues.

8. Use a thesaurus: Using a thesaurus can help you find stronger, more precise words to replace weaker ones.

9. Use strong verbs: Using strong verbs is an effective way to make your writing more engaging and impactful.

10. Simplify complex sentences: Finally, simplifying complex sentences can improve the clarity of your writing. Break long sentences into shorter ones or use conjunctions to connect ideas.

Remember, editing your memoir stories is an important part of the writing process. By following these tips and hacks, you can improve the quality of your writing and make your memoir the best it can be. So, let's get to editing – you've got this!

Legal and Ethical Considerations

Understanding Libel and Defamation

First, let's talk about the legal considerations. It's important to remember that while you have the freedom to write about your own experiences, you must also respect the privacy and rights of others. This means avoiding libel, defamation, invasion of privacy, and copyright infringement.

Defamation is when you make a false statement that harms someone's reputation. So, unless you have solid evidence to back up what you're saying, it's best to avoid making accusations.

Invasion of privacy is when you share information that someone has a reasonable expectation of keeping private. This includes details about someone's health, finances, and personal relationships. So, be sure to get permission from the people you're writing about before sharing any personal information.

Copyright infringement is when you use someone else's work without their permission. This includes using song lyrics, quotes, and images without proper attribution.

Now, let's talk about **ethical considerations**. As a writer, you have a responsibility to be honest and transparent with your readers. This means avoiding exaggeration, misrepresentation, and plagiarism.

Exaggeration is when you embellish the truth for dramatic effect. While some degree of creative license is acceptable in memoir writing, it's important to stay true to the facts as much as possible.

Misrepresentation is when you intentionally mislead your readers. This includes changing details about people or events to fit your narrative. Always strive for accuracy in your writing.

Plagiarism is when you use someone else's work without giving them credit. This includes using ideas, words, or phrases from another source without proper attribution.

Now that you have the basic understanding of some of the terms, let's talk about how you can avoid libel, defamation or other infractions in your memoir? Here are the top ten ways:

1. **Stick to the truth:** The best way to avoid libel and defamation is to stick to the truth. Don't embellish or exaggerate for dramatic effect.

2. **Change names and identifying details:** If you're worried about harming someone's reputation, consider changing their name or other identifying details in your memoir.

3. **Get permission:** If you plan to share private or personal information about someone in your memoir, get their permission first.

4. **Be cautious with criticism:** If you plan to criticize someone in your memoir, make sure your criticism is fair and based on facts.

5. **Be careful with humor:** Jokes can be misinterpreted or taken out of context, so make sure any humorous anecdotes in your memoir are in good taste and won't be seen as offensive or hurtful.

6. **Use caution with sensitive topics:** When writing about sensitive topics like politics or religion, be mindful of how your words might be perceived by others.

7. **Fact-check everything:** Make sure you fact-check all the information in your memoir to ensure that it's accurate and not defamatory.

8. **Consult a lawyer:** If you're unsure about whether something you've written might be considered libelous or defamatory, consider consulting a lawyer who specializes in publishing law.

9. **Be prepared to defend your work**: If someone decides to take legal action against you for something you've written in your memoir, be prepared to defend your work and prove that your statements are truthful and not defamatory.

10. **Use your judgment:** Ultimately, the best way to avoid libel and defamation in your memoir is to use your judgment and be mindful of how your words might affect others.

Remember, understanding your own rights and where the lines are drawn is an important part of writing your memoir. Not only is it important, but it's also your responsibility, so please take it seriously. You want to be fully authentic and honest about your own story without harming others.

By doing your own additional research, following these tips and being mindful of how your words might affect others, you can tell your story in a way that is both honest and respectful. So, let's get to writing – but let's do it responsibly!

NOTE: I am not an attorney, nor do I share this section of information to offer legal advice. It's intended to help start your own research toward a issue-free memoir. I advise you to do your own research and consult an attorney.

Protecting Privacy and Obtaining Permission

Now we're going to talk about an important topic when it comes to writing a personal memoir – protecting privacy and obtaining permission.

When you're writing a memoir, it's important to remember that you have a responsibility to protect the privacy of the people in your life. While you have the right to tell your story, you must also respect the rights of others. So, how can you avoid violating someone's privacy in your memoir? Here are the top ten ways:

1. **Obtain permission:** If you plan to include information about someone in your memoir, get their permission first.

2. **Change names and identifying details:** If you're worried about violating someone's privacy, consider changing their name or other identifying details in your memoir.

3. **Be cautious with sensitive information:** When sharing sensitive information about someone, be mindful of how it might affect them and their loved ones.

4. Use discretion with personal information: Avoid sharing personal information about someone that isn't relevant to your story.

5. Consider the impact on others: Before sharing information about someone in your memoir, consider how it might impact their reputation or personal life.

6. Stick to the facts: When sharing information about someone in your memoir, stick to the facts and avoid speculation or exaggeration.

7. Be respectful: When writing about someone in your memoir, be respectful and avoid making negative or hurtful statements.

8. Avoid stereotypes: When writing about people of different races, genders, or cultures, avoid using stereotypes or making broad generalizations.

9. Consult a lawyer: If you're unsure about whether something you've written might be considered a violation of someone's privacy, consider consulting a lawyer who specializes in publishing law.

10. Use your judgment: Ultimately, the best way to protect privacy in your memoir is to use your judgment and be mindful of how your words might affect others.

Balancing truth and fiction

Now we're going to talk about another important topic when it comes to writing a personal memoir – balancing truth and fiction.

When you're writing a memoir, it can be tempting to take some creative liberties with the truth in order to make your story more interesting or exciting. However, it's important to remember that you have a responsibility to be truthful and accurate in your writing. So, how can you avoid crossing the line into fiction in your memoir? Here are the top ten ways:

1. **Stick to the facts:** The best way to avoid fiction in your memoir is to stick to the facts. Don't embellish or exaggerate for dramatic effect.

2. **Be honest about your emotions:** While you should stick to the facts, you can still be honest about your emotions and how you felt during certain events.

3. **Use descriptive language:** You can make your story more interesting without making things up by using descriptive language to bring your experiences to life.

4. **Be honest about your perspective:** Remember that your memoir is just one perspective on the events

you're describing. Be honest about your point of view, but also be open to other perspectives.

5. **Avoid making assumptions:** Don't make assumptions about what other people were thinking or feeling unless you have evidence to support your claims.

6. **Fact-check everything:** Make sure you fact-check all the information in your memoir to ensure that it's accurate and truthful.

7. **Consult other sources:** If you're unsure about a particular fact or event, consider consulting other sources to confirm the information.

8. **Be transparent about any changes you make:** If you do make changes to the facts in your memoir, be transparent about what you've changed and why.

9. **Use your judgment:** Ultimately, the best way to balance truth and fiction in your memoir is to use your judgment and be mindful of how your words might be perceived by others.

10. **Consider the impact on others:** Before sharing information in your memoir, consider how it might impact the people in your life and their reputations.

Remember, you have a responsibility to balance truth and fiction in a way that is both honest and engaging. By following these tips and being mindful of how your words might affect others, you can tell your story in a way that is both truthful and respectful. So, let's get to writing – but let's watch our balance!

Top 10 Tips for Navigating Legal and Ethical Issues

Let's talk about an important topic when it comes to writing a personal memoir – navigating legal and ethical issues.

When you're writing a memoir, there are a number of legal and ethical issues that you need to be aware of. From copyright infringement to libel to invasion of privacy, there are many pitfalls to avoid. So, how can you navigate these issues and avoid legal trouble? Here are the top ten tips:

1. **Understand the law:** Familiarize yourself with the relevant laws and regulations governing publishing, copyright, and defamation.

2. **Obtain permissions:** If you plan to use quotes, lyrics, or other copyrighted material in your memoir, be sure to obtain the necessary permissions.

3. **Protect privacy:** Be mindful of the privacy of the people in your life and take steps to protect their identities and personal information.

4. **Avoid libel:** Don't make false statements about people in your memoir that could be considered defamatory.

5. Use disclaimers: Consider including a disclaimer at the beginning of your memoir to make it clear that your story is your own perspective.

6. Be respectful: When writing about people in your memoir, be respectful and avoid making negative or hurtful statements.

7. Consult a lawyer: If you're unsure about whether something you've written might be considered a violation of someone's rights, consider consulting a lawyer.

8. Fact-check everything: Make sure that all the information in your memoir is accurate and truthful.

9. Be transparent: If you do make changes to the facts in your memoir, be transparent about what you've changed and why.

10. Use your judgment: Ultimately, the best way to navigate legal and ethical issues in your memoir is to use your judgment and be mindful of how your words might be perceived by others.

Remember, you can tell your story in a way that is both engaging and legally sound. So, let's get to writing – but let's do it responsibly!

Publishing Your Memoir

Pros and Cons of Publishing versus Keeping it Private

Let's talk about a big decision that many memoir writers face – whether to publish their work or keep it private.

First, let's talk about the pros of publishing your memoir:

1. **Sharing your story:** By publishing your memoir, you have the opportunity to share your story with a wider audience and potentially inspire and connect with others.

2. **Validation:** Seeing your memoir in print can be incredibly validating and satisfying and can help you feel a sense of accomplishment.

3. **Feedback:** Publishing your memoir allows you to receive feedback from readers, which can help you improve your writing and gain insights into how your story is perceived.

4. **Potential Financial gain:** If your memoir is successful, you can potentially earn money from book sales and speaking engagements.

5. **Legacy:** By publishing your memoir, you're creating a permanent record of your life story that can be passed down to future generations.

Now, let's talk about the cons of publishing your memoir:

1. **Privacy:** By publishing your memoir, you may be giving up some of your privacy and exposing yourself and your loved ones to public scrutiny.

2. **Criticism:** Publishing your memoir also opens you up to criticism and negative reviews, which can be difficult to handle.

3. **Legal issues:** As we've discussed before, publishing a memoir comes with legal and ethical considerations that need to be carefully navigated.

4. **Rejection:** There's always a chance that your memoir won't be successful, which can be disappointing and demotivating.

5. **Pressure:** The pressure of putting your personal story out into the world can be intense and can lead to anxiety and stress.

Now, let's talk about the pros of keeping your memoir private:

1. **Control:** By keeping your memoir private, you have complete control over who sees it and how it's shared.

2. **Privacy:** You can maintain your privacy and the privacy of your loved ones by keeping your story within your inner circle.

3. **Less pressure:** Without the pressure of public scrutiny, you can focus solely on telling your story in the way that feels most true to you.

4. **Personal satisfaction:** Even if you don't share your memoir with the world, the act of writing it can be incredibly satisfying and healing.

5. **Emotional safety:** Sharing your personal story can be emotionally taxing, and keeping your memoir private can help protect your emotional well-being.

And finally, let's talk about the cons of keeping your memoir private:

1. **Missed opportunities**: By keeping your memoir private, you may miss out on opportunities to connect with others and share your story.

2. **Lack of validation:** Without the external validation that comes with publishing, you may feel less confident in your writing and less sure of your story's impact.

3. **No feedback:** Without sharing your memoir with others, you won't receive the feedback that can help you improve your writing and gain insights into your story.

4. **No financial gain:** Keeping your memoir private means you won't earn any money from book sales or speaking engagements.

5. **Missed legacy:** Without publishing, your memoir may not have the same lasting impact or be passed down to future generations.

Ultimately, the decision is a personal one that will depend on your goals, values, and comfort level. But remember, whether you choose to share your story with the world or keep it close to your heart, your story is valid and deserves to be told.

Traditional vs. Self-Publishing

Now, let's talk about a decision that many memoir writers face – whether to publish traditionally or self-publish.

First, let's talk about the pros of traditional publishing:

1. **Credibility:** Traditional publishing can give your memoir more credibility and help you gain recognition as a writer.

2. **Professional editing:** Publishers often provide professional editing services, which can help improve the quality of your writing.

3. **Marketing support:** Traditional publishers have marketing departments that can help promote your book and increase its visibility.

4. **Distribution:** Traditional publishers have established distribution networks that can help get your book into bookstores and other retail outlets.

5. **Advance payment:** Traditional publishers often pay an advance to the author, which can provide financial support while you work on your memoir.

Now, let's talk about the cons of traditional publishing:

1. **Limited control:** With traditional publishing, the publisher has the final say on everything from the cover design to the content of your memoir.

2. **Slow process:** The traditional publishing process can take a long time, with the potential for rejection and delays along the way.

3. **Royalties:** Traditional publishers often take a large percentage of the book's royalties, leaving the author with a smaller share of the profits.

4. **Fewer opportunities:** Traditional publishers only publish a limited number of books each year, so the competition for publication can be intense.

5. **Contract terms:** The terms of a traditional publishing contract can be complex and may limit your ability to make changes to your memoir.

Now, let's talk about the pros of self-publishing:

1. **Control:** Self-publishing gives you complete control over every aspect of your memoir, from the cover design to the content.

2. **Faster process:** With self-publishing, you can get your memoir into the hands of readers much more quickly than with traditional publishing.

3. **Royalties:** With self-publishing, you keep a larger percentage of the book's royalties, which can mean more money in your pocket.

4. **More opportunities:** Self-publishing allows you to bypass the traditional gatekeepers and get your memoir into the hands of readers who might not have found it otherwise.

5. **Flexible contract terms:** With self-publishing, you can choose the terms of your contract and make changes to your memoir as needed.

Now, let's talk about the cons of self-publishing:

1. **Limited credibility:** Self-published books may be seen as less credible than traditionally published books, which can make it harder to gain recognition as a writer.

2. **Limited marketing support:** Without a publisher's marketing department, self-published

authors may struggle to promote their books and reach a wider audience.

3. **No advance payment:** Self-publishing does not provide an advance payment, so you may need to fund the publication process yourself.

4. **Limited distribution:** Self-published books may be harder to get into bookstores and other retail outlets.

5. **Quality control:** With self-publishing, the responsibility for editing and proofreading falls entirely on the author, which can result in lower-quality writing.

Ultimately, the decision is a personal one that will depend on your goals, values, and preferences. But no matter which route you choose, remember that the most important thing is to share your story with the world.

Whether it's through a traditional publisher or self-publishing, your memoir deserves to be read and appreciated by others.

Creating a Book Proposal

Let's talk about the top ten steps and pro tips for creating a book proposal for your personal memoir.

1. **Start with a strong hook:** The first few sentences of your proposal should grab the reader's attention and make them want to keep reading. Think of it like the opening scene of a movie – it needs to be intriguing and memorable.

2. **Provide a summary of your memoir:** Give a brief overview of your memoir, including its central themes and main characters. This will help the reader understand what your memoir is about and what they can expect from it.

3. **Highlight your unique perspective:** What sets your memoir apart from others? What unique experiences and insights do you bring to the table? Be sure to emphasize what makes your memoir stand out.

4. **Include a sample chapter:** Including a sample chapter can give the reader a taste of your writing style and help them get a sense of what to expect from the rest of the book.

5. **Discuss your target audience:** Who do you envision reading your memoir? What demographic are

they in? Understanding your target audience can help publishers determine how to market your book.

6. **Provide a market analysis:** Do some research and identify other memoirs that are similar to yours. What sets your memoir apart? How does it fit into the current market?

7. **Include a marketing plan:** Publishers want to know that you're invested in promoting your book. Outline your plan for promoting your memoir, including any social media or advertising campaigns.

8. **Discuss your platform:** Do you have a blog or social media following? Have you been featured in any publications? Your platform can demonstrate to publishers that you have a built-in audience.

9. **Provide a list of endorsements:** Have any notable individuals or publications given your memoir positive reviews? Including these endorsements in your proposal can give publishers confidence in your book.

10. **Edit, edit, edit:** Finally, be sure to thoroughly edit your proposal. Spelling errors and typos can make it appear unprofessional, so take the time to make sure everything is polished and error-free.

The goal is to make your proposal stand out and convince publishers that your memoir is worth investing in. By following these steps and putting your best foot forward, you'll be one step closer to seeing your memoir in print.

Finding a Literary Agent

Today we're going to talk about the top ten steps and pro tips for finding a literary agent for traditional publishing for your personal memoir.

1. **Research potential agents:** Start by researching agents who represent memoirs. Look at their websites and social media profiles to get a sense of their tastes and interests.

2. **Build a list of potential agents:** Make a list of potential agents who represent memoirs that are similar to yours. Be sure to include their contact information and submission guidelines.

3. **Personalize your query letter:** When submitting your query letter, be sure to personalize it for each agent. Mention why you're interested in working with them specifically.

4. **Follow submission guidelines:** Be sure to carefully read and follow each agent's submission guidelines. Failure to do so can result in your query being rejected before it's even read.

5. **Be patient:** Finding the right agent can take time. Be patient and don't give up if you don't hear back immediately.

6. Attend writing conferences and workshops: Attending writing conferences and workshops can give you the opportunity to meet agents in person and pitch your memoir directly to them.

7. Build your platform: Having a strong platform can make you more attractive to agents. Build your online presence by blogging, guest posting, and engaging with your audience on social media.

8. Join writing groups: Joining writing groups can give you the opportunity to network with other writers and potentially make connections with agents.

9. Be prepared to revise: If an agent expresses interest in your memoir, be prepared to make revisions based on their feedback.

10. Keep submitting: If you don't find an agent right away, don't give up. Keep submitting to new agents and revising your query letter until you find the right fit.

There you have it – the top ten steps and pro tips for finding a literary agent for traditional publishing for your personal memoir. Remember, finding the right agent can be a long and difficult process, but it's worth it if it means getting your memoir published. Keep pushing forward and don't give up on your dreams!

Top 10 Tips for Successfully Publishing Your Memoir

Now let's start to wrap up the lesson and yes, the course as we talk about the top ten steps and pro tips for self-publishing your personal memoir.

1. **Edit, edit, edit:** Before you even think about self-publishing, be sure to thoroughly edit your memoir. Get feedback from beta readers and hire a professional editor if possible.

2. **Choose a platform:** There are several self-publishing platforms to choose from, including Amazon Kindle Direct Publishing, Barnes & Noble Press, and IngramSpark. Research each platform to determine which is best for you.

3. **Create a cover design:** Your memoir's cover is the first thing readers will see, so it's important to make a good impression. Consider hiring a professional designer or using a pre-made template.

4. **Format your manuscript:** Formatting your manuscript for e-book and print versions can be a daunting task, but there are several tools and resources available to help.

5. **Set a realistic budget:** Self-publishing can be expensive, so it's important to set a realistic budget for expenses like editing, cover design, and marketing.

6. **Create a marketing plan:** You'll need to take an active role in promoting your memoir. Consider using social media, advertising, and book bloggers to get the word out.

7. **Choose a launch date:** Determine when you want to release your memoir and start planning your launch strategy well in advance.

8. **Get reviews:** Reviews can be a powerful tool for promoting your memoir. Reach out to book bloggers and other reviewers to request reviews.

9. **Engage with your readers:** Once your memoir is published, engage with your readers by responding to reviews and creating a sense of community around your book.

10. **Keep writing:** Finally, don't stop writing just because you've self-published one memoir. Keep honing your craft and creating new stories to share with the world.

Conclusion

Well, that brings us to the end of our course on writing a personal memoir. I hope you've learned a thing or two about the writing process and how to craft a compelling and memorable memoir.

If you enjoyed this course, please like and follow us for more great videos on writing and storytelling. We have plenty of other courses and tutorials to help you improve your craft and achieve your writing goals.

And if you're feeling inspired to start writing your memoir, remember to take it one step at a time. Whether you choose to pursue traditional publishing or self-publishing, there's a path that's right for you.

Thank you for joining me on this learning journey. I hope you'll subscribe to our channel on YouTube, join the writing group on Facebook, and consider letting us help you with your very own personal memoir.

The I Remember When memoir project provides you with a preformatted template, we have dozens of professionally designed book covers that can be customized to become your very own, monthly live sessions for Q&A as well as shoutouts for those who are making progress on their memoirs!

The I Remember When Pro project also provides basic editing to help you through the toughest aspects of the process.

Plus, everyone in the US will get a copy of their book with the option of purchasing additional copies, or an eBook version to be shared freely as you choose.

Now that you know how to do the part that is inside you, consider allowing my team and I to help you with the stuff that no one enjoys!

Keep telling your story and sharing your voice with the world!

You can find information on the I Remember When project at https://www.writercertification.com/remember or join the free writing community at https://www.facebook.com/groups/aspiring

Let your creativity soar!

About the Author

Sydney founded the "I'm the Writer–Publishing Professional" certification program to properly train ghostwriters and freelancers to provide top-notch, income-generating services for their clients.

Through her experience as a publisher and someone who hires freelance writers, ghostwriters, and virtual assistants on a regular basis, she found that the market was flooded with applicants who had little or no skills to properly help a client.

Those who did have skills were diamonds in the rough, leaving her to recognize the intense need for a certification program that confirms that a graduate will have been verified to have completed all of the criteria needed to deliver quality stories and other deliverables such as graphics, videos, content creation, and general virtual assistance.

https://www.writercertification.com

Also From TLM Publishing House

FICTION -
Sydney Brown Presents Series
https -//www.amazon.com/dp/B0BSBT36HN
The Mall Cadet Series
https -//www.amazon.com/gp/product/B0B66MDK3T
All In or Nothing Series
https -//www.amazon.com/dp/B0B7FW9W8M
The 7 Wishes Series
https -//www.amazon.com/dp/B0B62XJY59
The Deception Series
https -//www.amazon.com/dp/B0B5RNQMF1
The Forbidden Love Series (18+)
https -//www.amazon.com/dp/B0B5SX24SX
NONFICTION -
How to Start It Series
https -//www.amazon.com/dp/B09Y2QHDPM

Ready to share your story with the world?

I'm the writer publishing professional certification program that will teach you how to craft a fiction story so you can become a ghostwriter, or share your own stories with the world.

For more info, go to [https -//www.writercertification.com](https://www.writercertification.com)